Pentatonic Scales
for Electric Bass
by Max Palermo

**A Practical Approach to the
Pentatonic Scales World for 4 and 5 String**

ISBN: 978-1-57424-247-8
SAN 683-8022

Cover photo courtesy of Ibanez Guitars and Basses

Cover Design by James Creative Group

Copyright © Max Palermo

Copyright © 2009 CENTERSTREAM Publishing, LLC
P.O. Box 17878 - Anaheim Hills, CA 92817

www.centerstream-usa.com

Contents

I am grateful to Patrizia for her never-ending love and support and my sincere thanks to Ron Middlebrook for believing in this project.

Introduction

Pentatonic scales are probably the most used scales in music. They are widely employed in jazz, rock, blues, fusion, pop, and practically in all kinds of music around the world. This fact makes the pentatonic scale a very important part of learning to play.

Simply put it consists of five notes within one octave, that's why it is also sometimes referred to as a five-tone scale or five-note scale. So, whereas a conventional scale consists entirely of steps, a pentatonic scale always contains some steps and some larger leaps to cover an octave in five steps, creating this way its distinctive sound characteristic.

This book focus on the most frequently used pentatonic scales, including the ethnic and the exotic scales.

Each scale in this reference guide is introduced by a brief summary showing the scale structure and construction, the main chords over which the scale works well and a list of relevant scales that, with their color and flavor affinities, give rise to a similar melodic effect with the same sound characteristics. The development over one and two octaves follows, together with fingerings and tablature for 4 and 5-string basses.

An effective use of these scales, joined to your own taste and feel, will certainly enrich your personal repertoire of patterns in every given musical situation improving your playing with new melodic hints.

Enjoy your playing!

THE Major Pentatonic scale

Construction

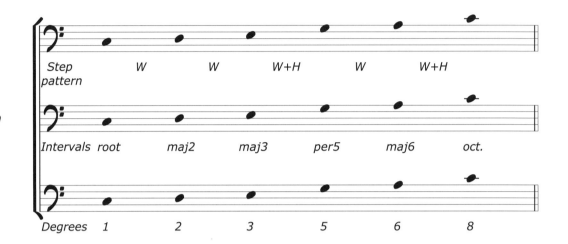

Step pattern		W	W	W+H	W	W+H	
Intervals	root	maj2	maj3	per5	maj6	oct.	
Degrees	1	2	3	5	6	8	

Chords

(Play the scale over these chords)

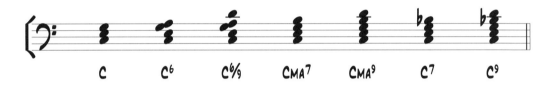

C   C6   C6/9   CMA7   CMA9   C7   C9

Related scales

(Scales with the same sound characteristics)

ionian, lydian, mixolydian, lydian dominant

One Octave Positions

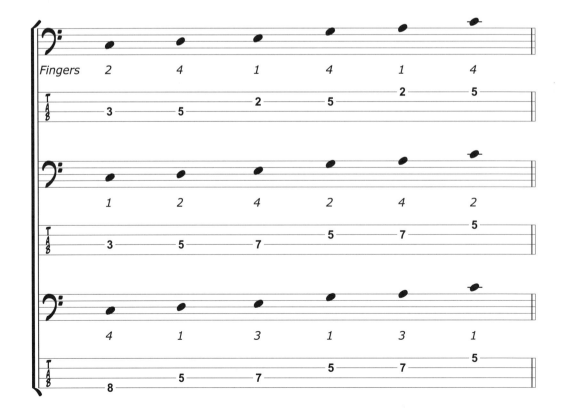

C Major Pentatonic

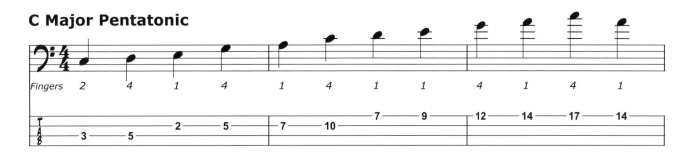

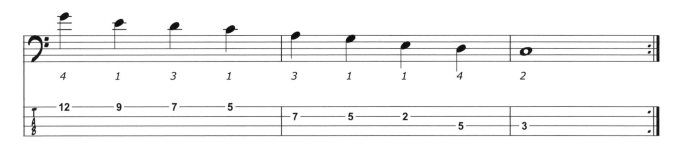

D Major Pentatonic

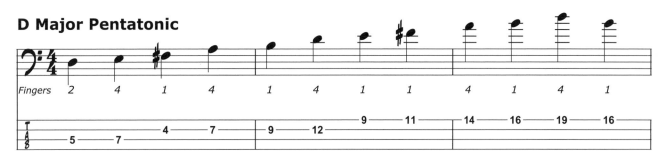

E Major Pentatonic

The Major Pentatonic scale

4-string positions

F Major Pentatonic

G Major Pentatonic

A Major Pentatonic

B Major Pentatonic

C Major Pentatonic

D Major Pentatonic

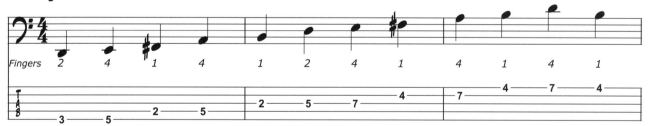

THE Dominant Pentatonic scale

Construction

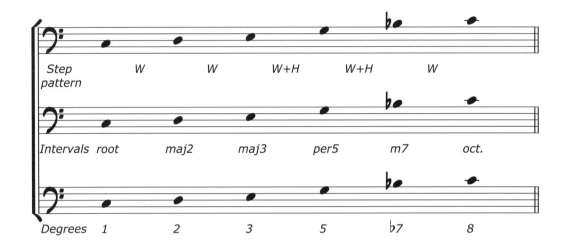

Step pattern		W	W	W+H	W+H	W

Intervals	root	maj2	maj3	per5	m7	oct.

Degrees	1	2	3	5	♭7	8

Chords
(Play the scale over these chords)

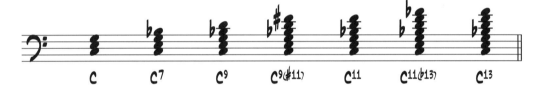

C   C⁷   C⁹   C⁹⁽♯¹¹⁾   C¹¹   C¹¹⁽♭¹³⁾   C¹³

Related scales
(Scales with the same sound characteristics)

mixolydian, lydian dominant, mixolydian b6, lydian minor

One Octave Positions

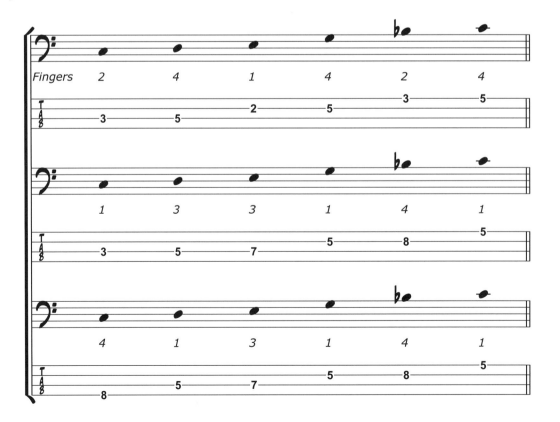

Fingers	2	4	1	4	2	4

	1	3	3	1	4	1

	4	1	3	1	4	1

C Dominant Pentatonic

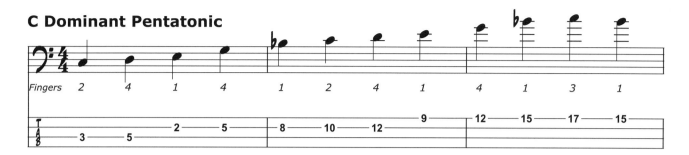

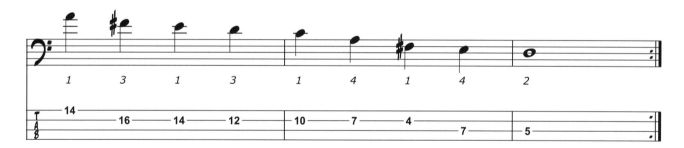

D Dominant Pentatonic

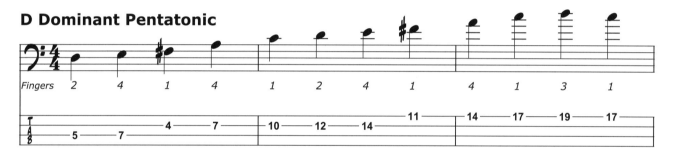

E Dominant Pentatonic

The Dominant Pentatonic scale

4-string positions

F Dominant Pentatonic

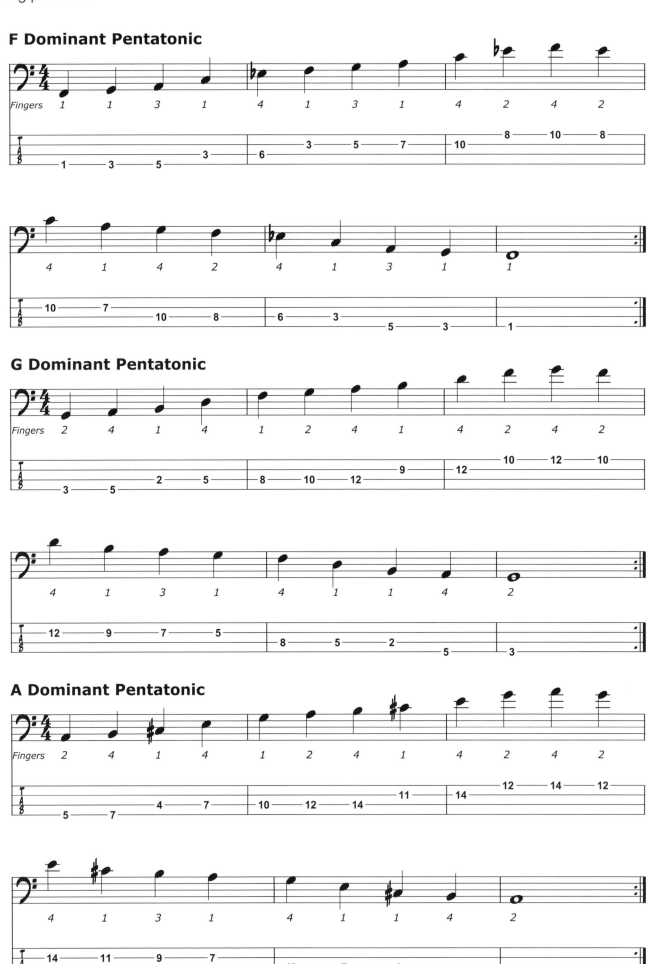

G Dominant Pentatonic

A Dominant Pentatonic

B Dominant Pentatonic

C Dominant Pentatonic

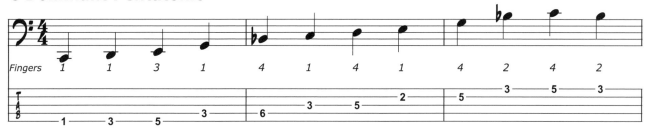

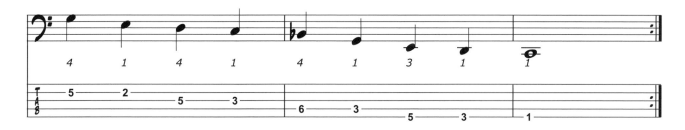

D Dominant Pentatonic

THE Chinese scale

Construction

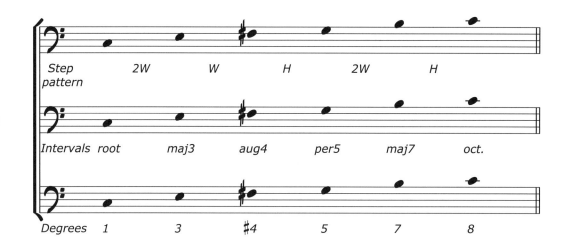

		Step pattern		2W	W	H	2W	H	

Intervals	root	maj3	aug4	per5	maj7	oct.

Degrees	1	3	#4	5	7	8

Chords
(Play the scale over these chords)

C   C⁶   C(add 9)   CMA7   CMA9(#11)   CMA13(#11)

Related scales
(Scales with the same sound characteristics)

lydian, harmonic minor - mode 6, marva and purvi (Indian ragas)

One Octave Positions

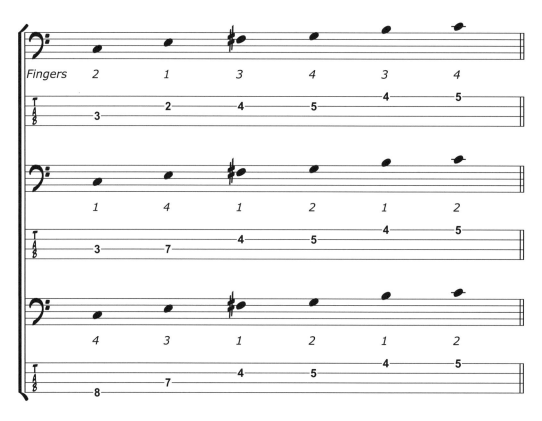

C Chinese

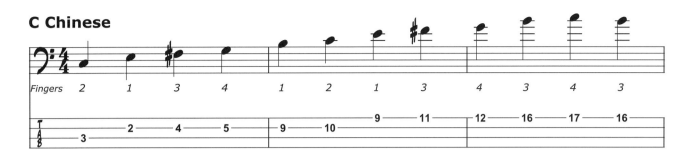

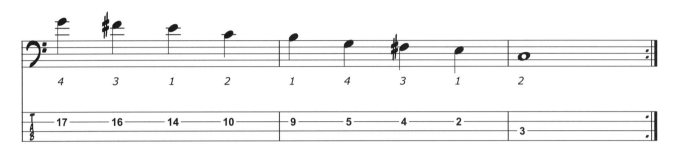

D Chinese

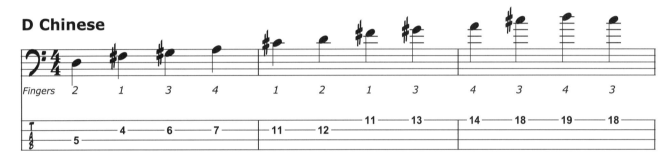

E Chinese

The Chinese scale

4-string positions

F Chinese

G Chinese

A Chinese

B Chinese

C Chinese

D Chinese

THE Indian scale

Construction

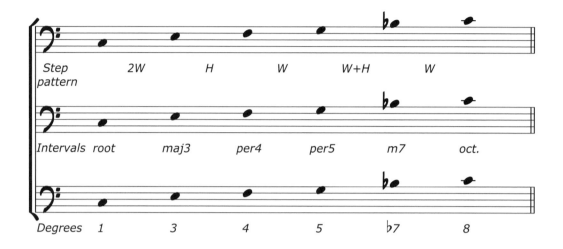

Step pattern		2W	H	W	W+H	W
Intervals	root	maj3	per4	per5	m7	oct.
Degrees	1	3	4	5	♭7	8

Chords

(Play the scale over these chords)

C   Csus⁴   C⁷   C⁷sus⁴   C⁹   C⁹sus⁴   C¹³sus⁴

Related scales

(Scales with the same sound characteristics)

mixolydian, mixolydian b6, Spanish gypsy

One Octave Positions

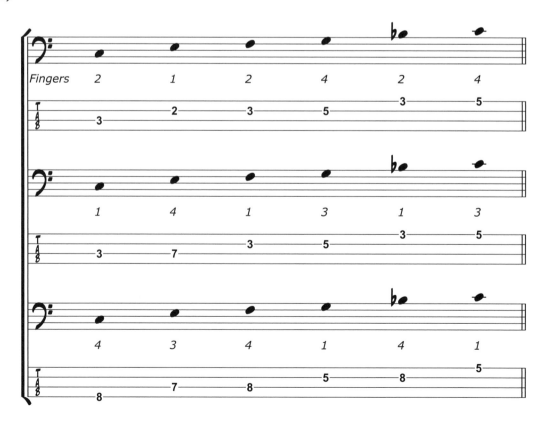

C Indian (Jog)

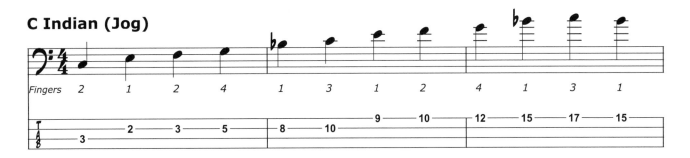

D Indian

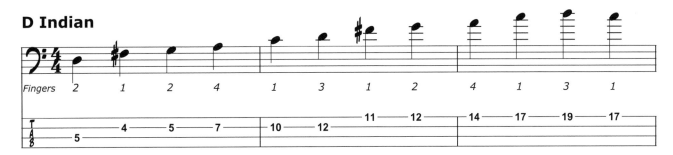

E Indian

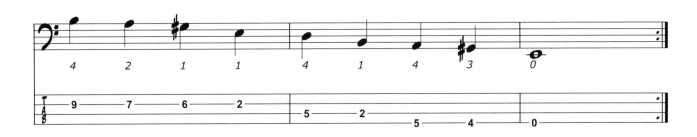

The Indian scale
4-string positions

F Indian

G Indian

G Indian

B Indian

C Indian

D Indian

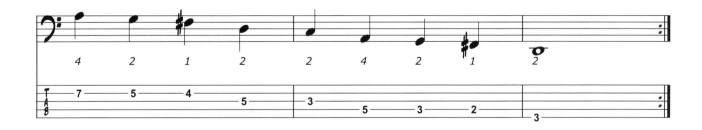

THE Major Pentatonic ♭6 scale

Construction

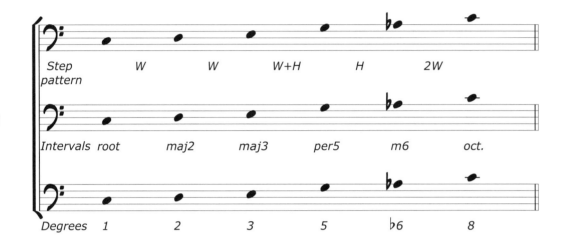

Step pattern		W	W	W+H	H	2W
Intervals	root	maj2	maj3	per5	m6	oct.
Degrees	1	2	3	5	♭6	8

Chords

(Play the scale over these chords)

C   C(ADD 9)   CMA7   CMA7(ADD ♭13)   CMA9   CMA9(ADD ♭13)

Related scales

(Scales with the same sound characteristics)

mixolydian b6, lydian minor

One Octave Positions

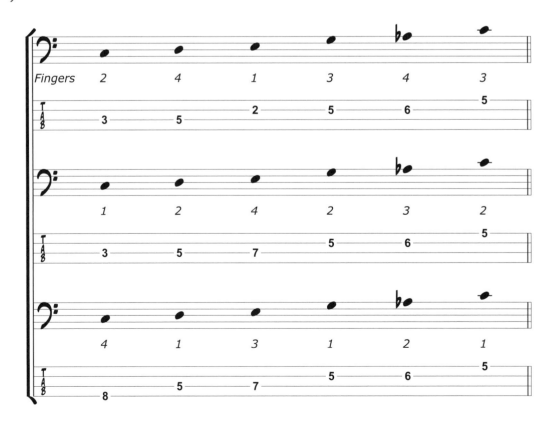

C Major Pentatonic b6

D Major Pentatonic b6

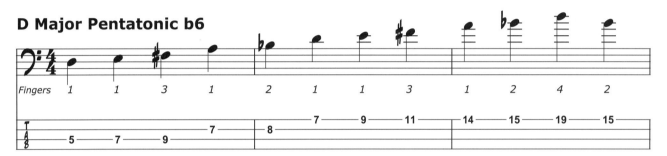

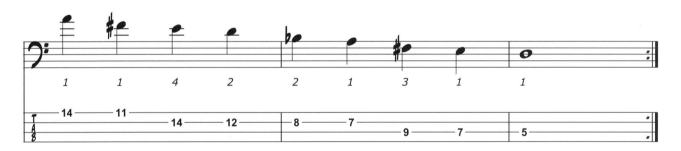

E Major Pentatonic b6

The Major Pentatonic ♭6 scale

4-string positions

F Major Pentatonic b6

G Major Pentatonic b6

A Major Pentatonic b6

B Major Pentatonic b6

C Major Pentatonic b6

D Major Pentatonic b6

THE Scriabin scale

Construction

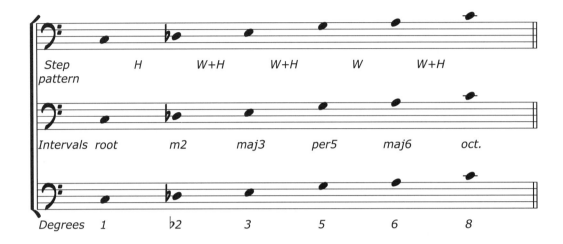

Step pattern	H	W+H	W+H	W	W+H

Intervals	root	m2	maj3	per5	maj6	oct.

Degrees	1	♭2	3	5	6	8

Chords

(Play the scale over these chords)

C   C⁶   C⁷   C7(♭9)   C7(add 13)   C13(♭9)

Related scales

(Scales with the same sound characteristics)

diminished h/w, Prometheus Neapolitan, marva (Indian raga)

One Octave Positions

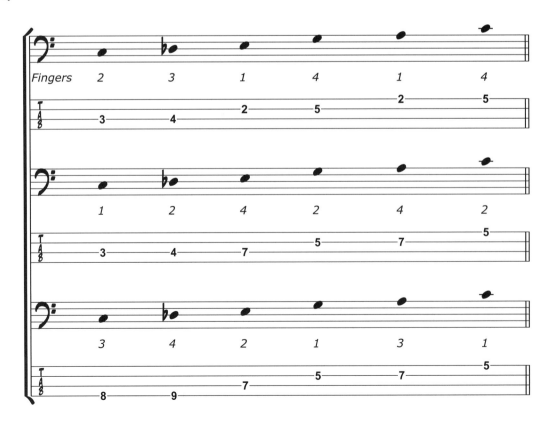

Fingers	2	3	1	4	1	4

	1	2	4	2	4	2

	3	4	2	1	3	1

C Scriabin

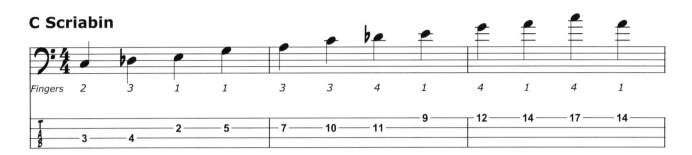

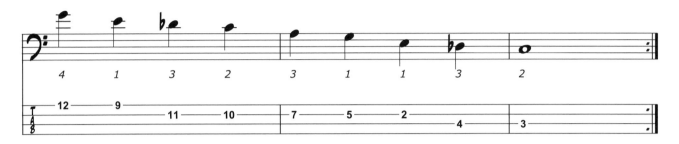

D Scriabin

E Scriabin

F Scriabin

G Scriabin

A Scriabin

B Scriabin

C Scriabin

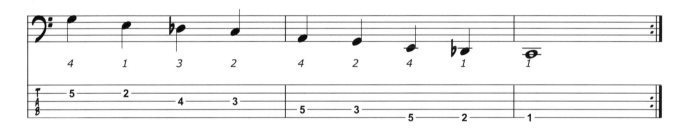

D Scriabin

THE Greek Arkaik scale

Construction

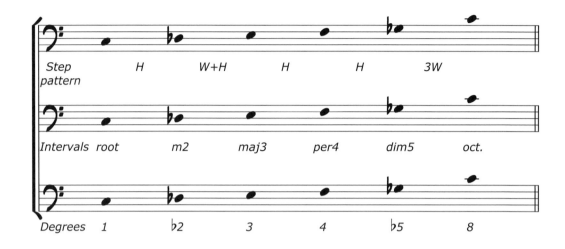

Step pattern		H	W+H	H	H	3W	
Intervals	root	m2	maj3	per4	dim5	oct.	
Degrees	1	b2	3	4	b5	8	

Chords

(Play the scale over these chords)

C(b5)   C7(b5)   C7(b5 b9)   C7(b5 b9 b13)

Related scales

(Scales with the same sound characteristics)

Spanish (eight-tone), double harmonic - mode 5, Persian

One Octave Positions

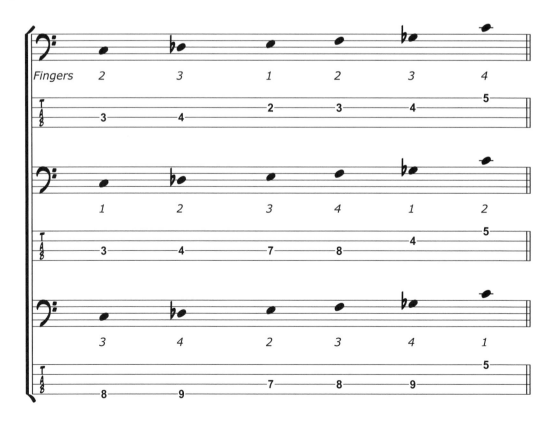

C Greek Arkaik

D Greek Arkaik

E Greek Arkaik

F Greek Arkaik

G Greek Arkaik

A Greek Arkaik

B Greek Arkaik

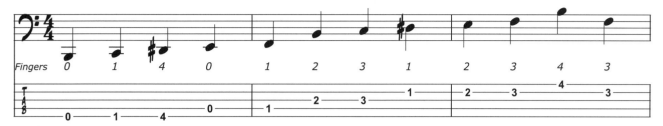

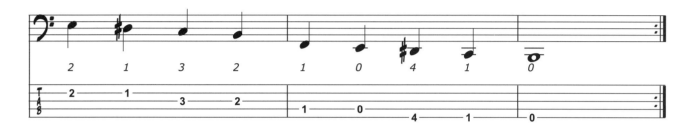

C Greek Arkaik

C Greek Arkaik

THE Minor Pentatonic scale

Construction

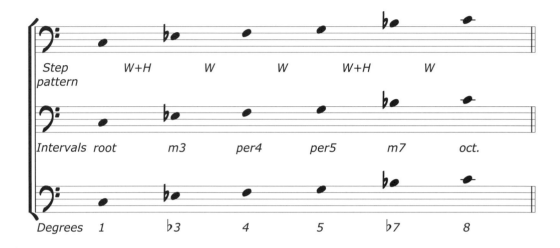

Step pattern		W+H	W	W	W+H	W
Intervals	root	m3	per4	per5	m7	oct.
Degrees	1	b3	4	5	b7	8

Chords

(Play the scale over these chords)

CM   CM6   CM7   CM9   CM9(ADD 13)   CM7(b9)   C7(#9)

Related scales

(Scales with the same sound characteristics)

dorian, phrygian, aeolian, dorian b2, blues

One Octave Positions

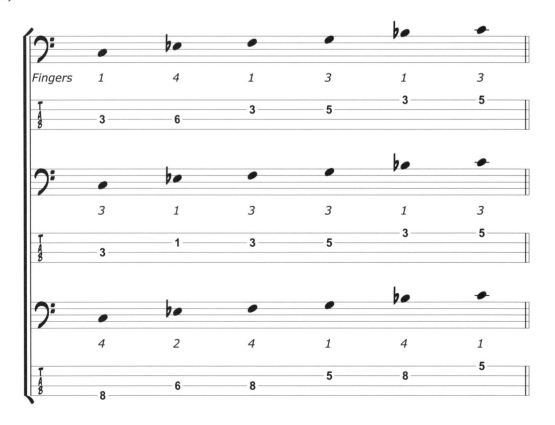

C Minor Pentatonic

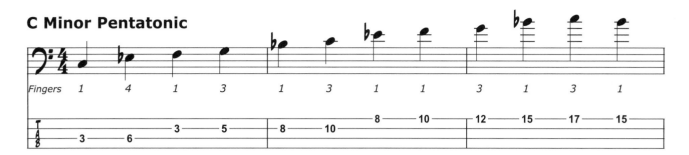

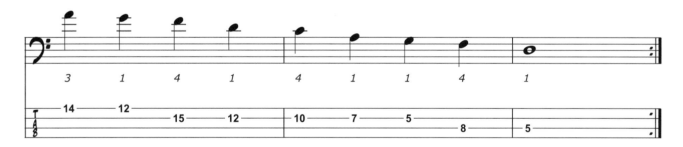

D Minor Pentatonic

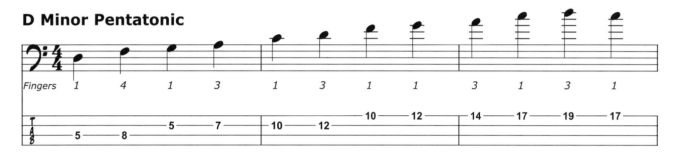

E Minor Pentatonic

4-string positions

F Minor Pentatonic

G Minor Pentatonic

A Minor Pentatonic

B Minor Pentatonic

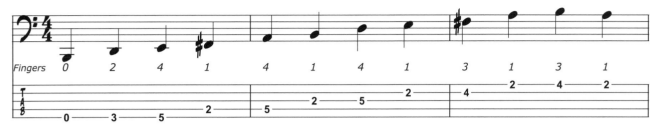

C Minor Pentatonic

D Minor Pentatonic

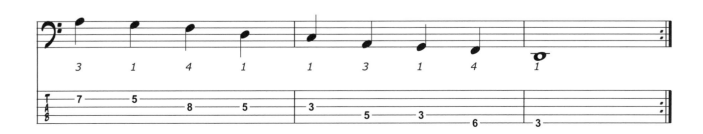

THE Man Gong scale

Construction

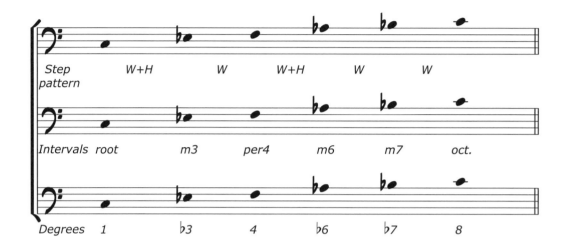

Step pattern		W+H		W		W+H		W		W	
Intervals	root		m3		per4		m6		m7		oct.
Degrees	1		♭3		4		♭6		♭7		8

Chords

(Play the scale over these chords)

CM   CM7   CM9   CM9(add ♭13)   CM7(♭9)   CM7(add 11)   CM11

Related scales

(Scales with the same sound characteristics)

phrygian, aeolian, locrian, Spanish (eight-note)

One Octave Positions

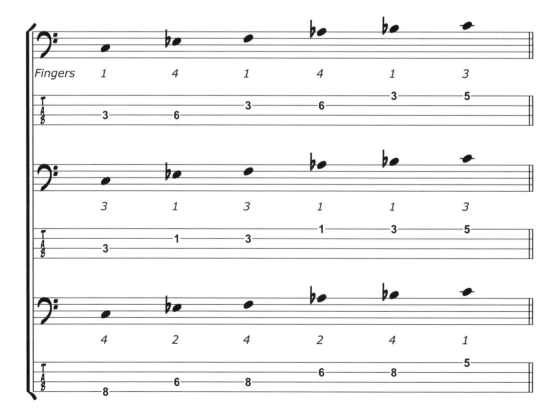

C Man Gong (Major Pentatonic - Mode 3)

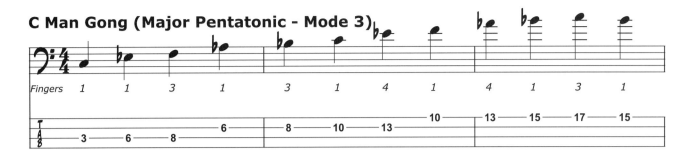

D Man Gong

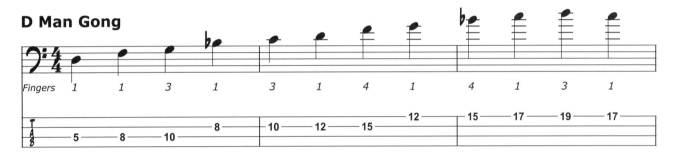

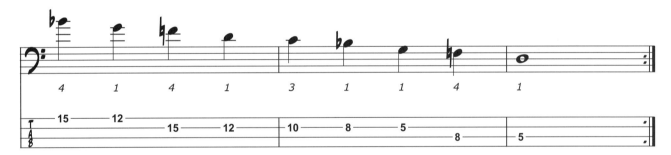

E Man Gong

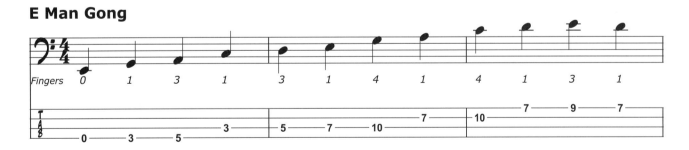

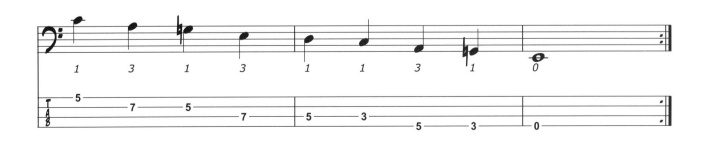

The Man Gong scale
4-string positions

F Man Gong

G Man Gong

A Man Gong

B Man Gong

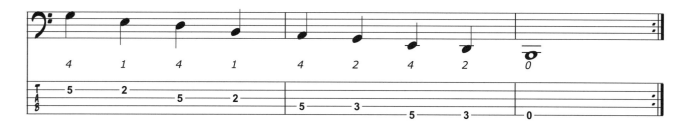

C Man Gong

D Man Gong

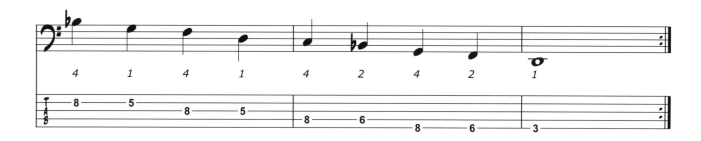

THE Hibrid scale

Construction

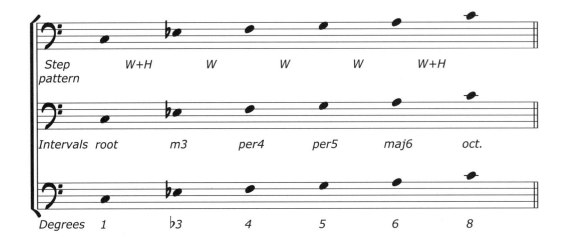

Step pattern	W+H	W	W	W	W+H	
Intervals	root	m3	per4	per5	maj6	oct.
Degrees	1	♭3	4	5	6	8

Chords

(Play the scale over these chords)

CM   CM6   CM6/9   CM7   CM7(add 11)   CM7(add 13)   CM11

Related scales

(Scales with the same sound characteristics)

dorian, melodic minor, dorian b2, blues, Neapolitan

One Octave Positions

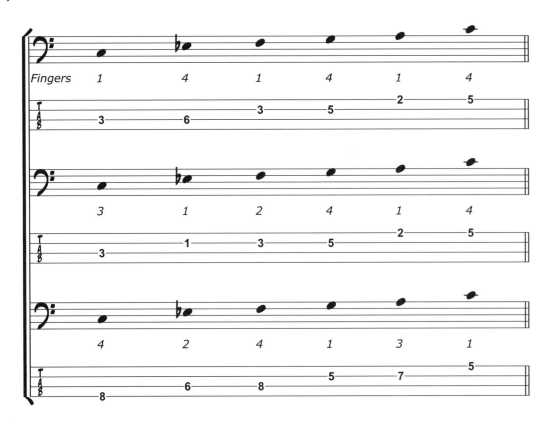

C Hibrid

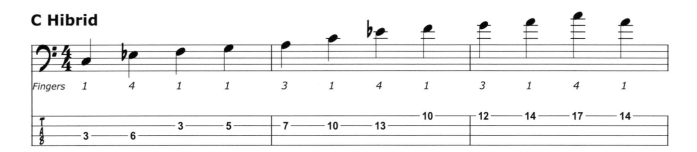

D Hibrid

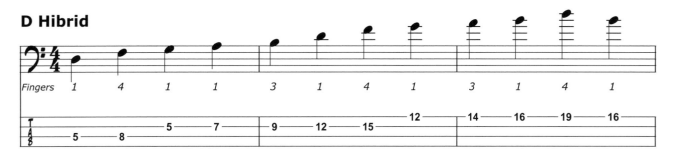

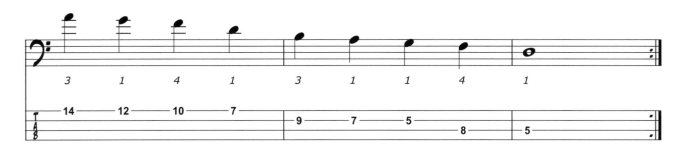

E Hibrid

The Hibrid scale

4-string positions

F Hibrid

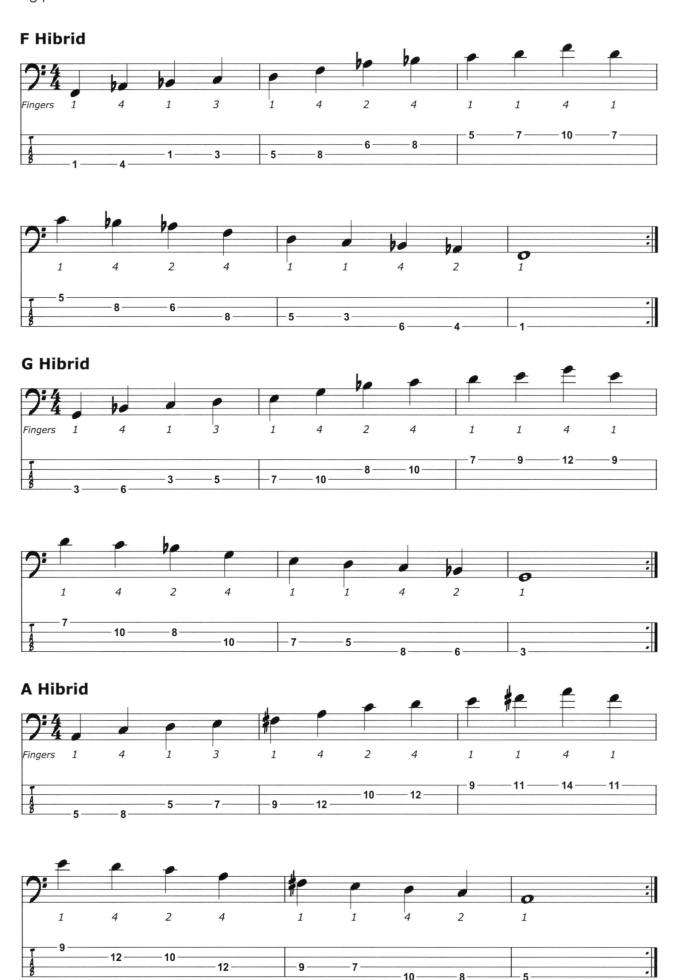

G Hibrid

A Hibrid

44

B Hibrid

C Hibrid

D Hibrid

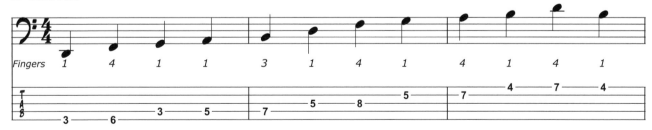

THE Pigmy scale

Construction

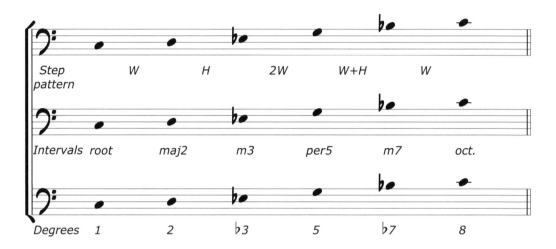

Step pattern		W	H	2W	W+H	W

Intervals	root	maj2	m3	per5	m7	oct.

Degrees	1	2	♭3	5	♭7	8

Chords
(Play the scale over these chords)

CM   CM(ADD 9)   CM6   C7   CM9

Related scales
(Scales with the same sound characteristics)

dorian, aeolian, dorian #4, blues

One Octave Positions

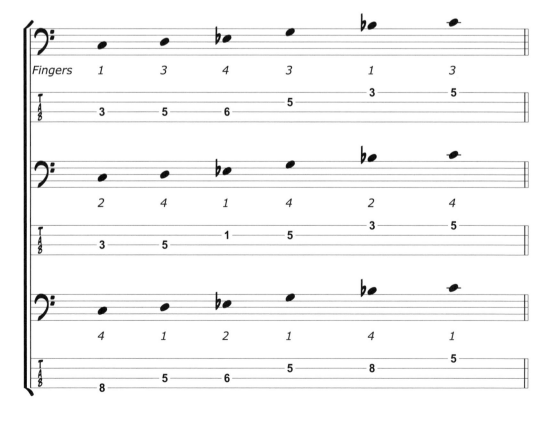

C Pigmy

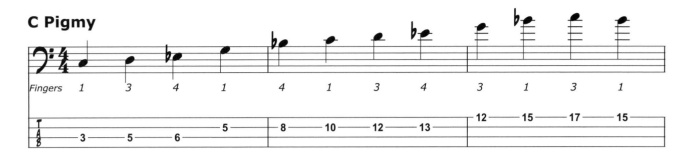

D Pigmy

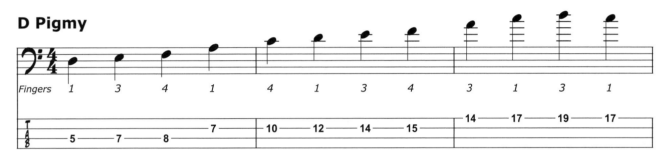

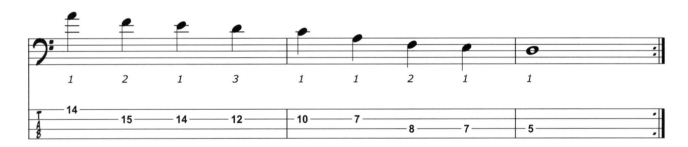

E Pigmy

The Pigmy scale

4-string positions

F Pigmy

G Pigmy

A Pigmy

B Pigmy

C Pigmy

D Pigmy

THE Kumoi scale

Construction

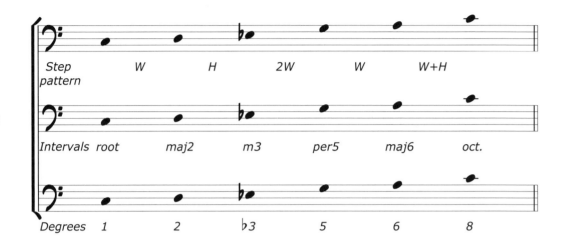

Step pattern		W	H	2W	W	W+H	
Intervals	root	maj2	m3	per5	maj6	oct.
Degrees	1	2	♭3	5	6	8

Chords

(Play the scale over these chords)

CM   CM⁷   CM⁹   CM⁶   CM⁶/₉   CM⁷(ADD 13)   CM¹³

Related scales

(Scales with the same sound characteristics)

dorian, melodic minor, dorian #4

One Octave Positions

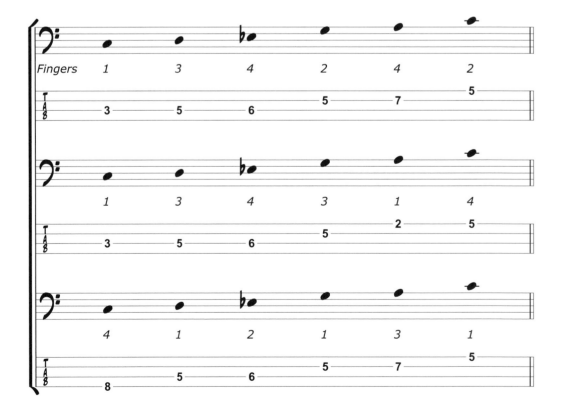

50

C Kumoi

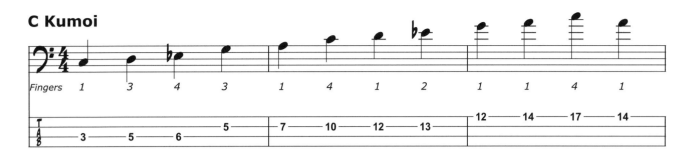

D Kumoi

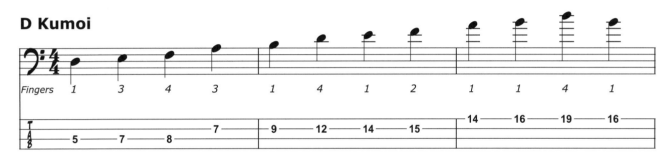

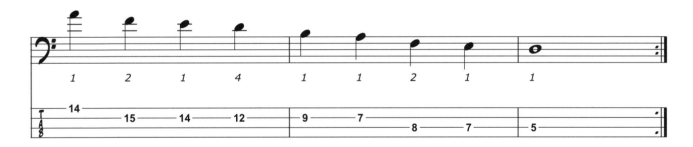

E Kumoi

The Kumoi scale

4-string positions

F Kumoi

G Kumoi

A Kumoi

B Kumoi

C Kumoi

D Kumoi

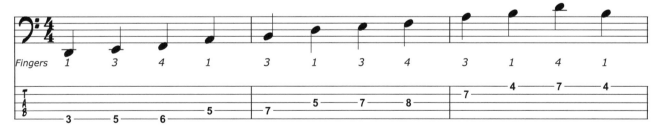

THE Hirajoshi scale

Construction

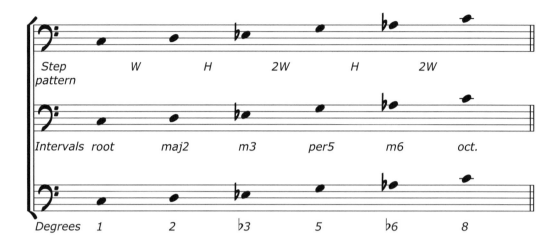

Step pattern		W	H	2W	H	2W
Intervals	root	maj2	m3	per5	m6	oct.
Degrees	1	2	b3	5	b6	8

Chords

(Play the scale over these chords)

Cм   Cм(add 9)   Cм(b6)   Cм7   Cм7(b6)   Cм9   Cм9(add b13)

Related scales

(Scales with the same sound characteristics)

aeolian, harmonic minor, Ungarian minor

One Octave Positions

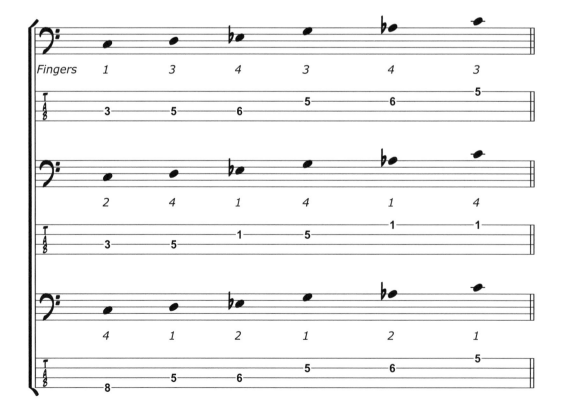

C Hirajoshi

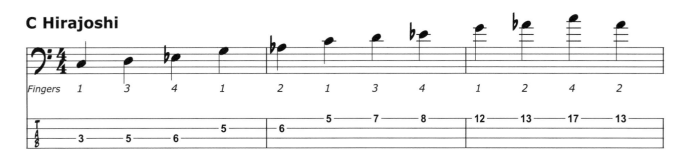

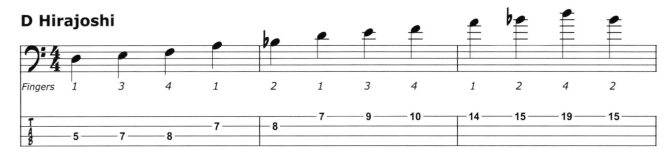

D Hirajoshi

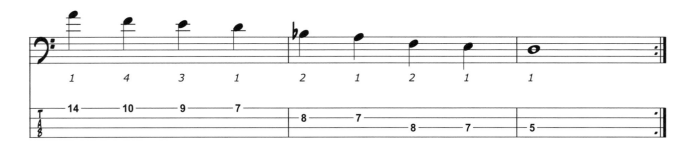

E Hirajoshi

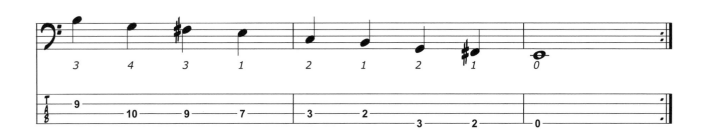

The Hirajoshi scale
4-string positions

F Hirajoshi

G Hirajoshi

A Hirajoshi

B Hirajoshi

C Hirajoshi

D Hirajoshi

Construction

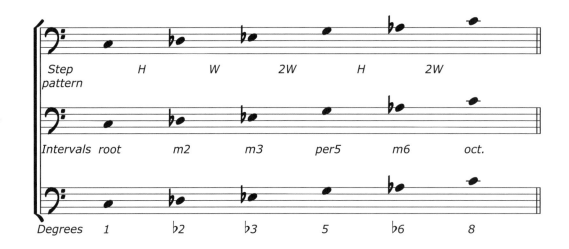

Step pattern		H	W	2W	H	2W	
Intervals	root	m2	m3	per5	m6	oct.	
Degrees	1	b2	b3	5	b6	8	

Chords

(Play the scale over these chords)

CM   CM7   C7sus4   CM7(b9)   CM7(addb9 b13)

Related scales

(Scales with the same sound characteristics)

phrygian, Neapolitan minor, todi (Indian raga)

One Octave Positions

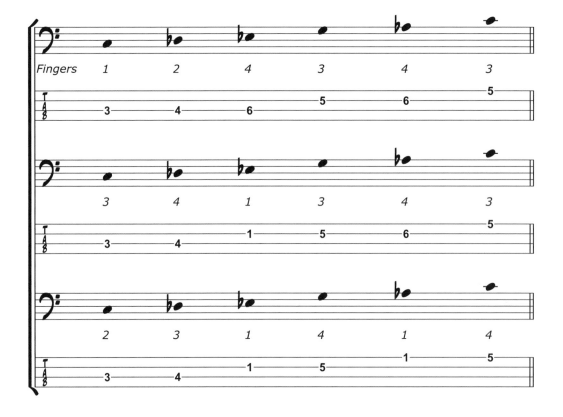

C Pelog

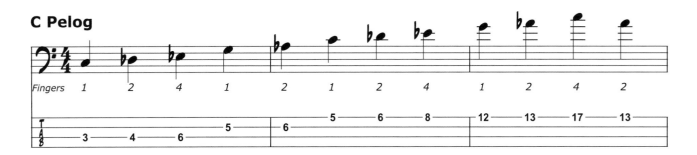

D Pelog

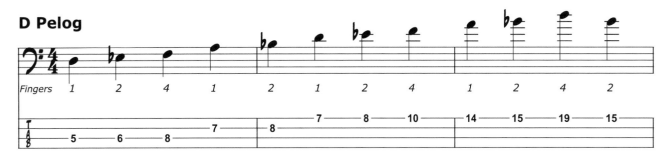

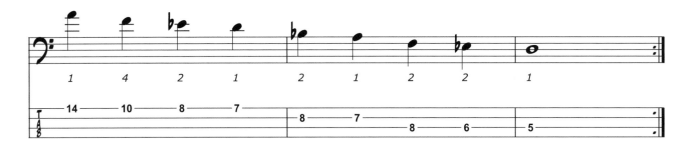

E Pelog

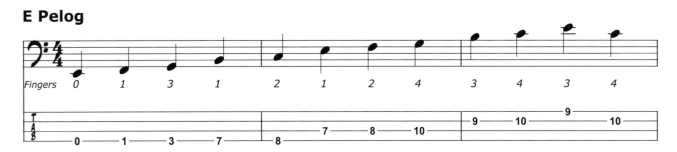

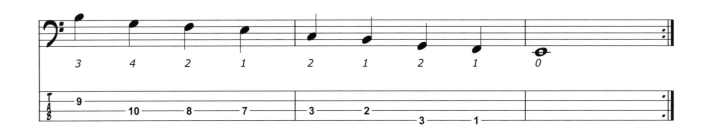

The Pelog scale

4-string positions

B Pelog

C Pelog

D Pelog

THE Ritusen scale

Construction

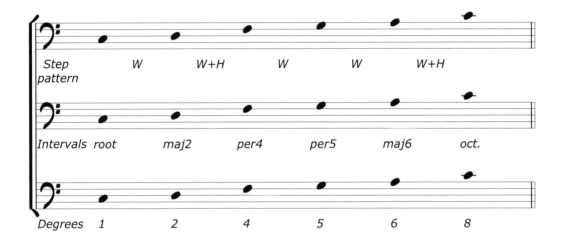

		W	W+H	W	W	W+H	
Step pattern							
Intervals	root	maj2	per4	per5	maj6	oct.	
Degrees	1	2	4	5	6	8	

Chords
(Play the scale over these chords)

CM   Csus⁴   CM⁶   CM⁷   C⁷sus⁴   C¹¹   CM¹³

Related scales
(Scales with the same sound characteristics)

ionian, dorian, mixolydian, melodic minor

One Octave Positions

Fingers	2	4	2	4	1	4

	1	3	1	1	3	1

	4	1	4	1	3	1

C Ritusen (Major Pentatonic - Mode 4)

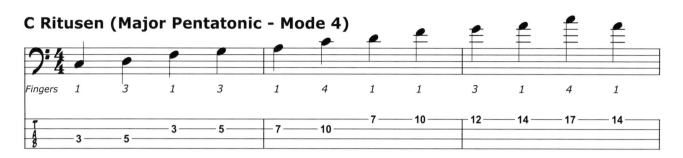

D Ritusen

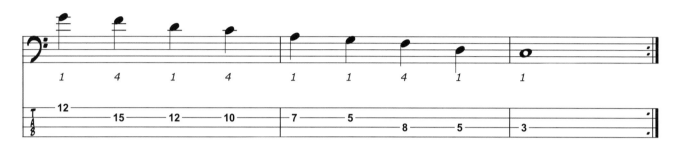

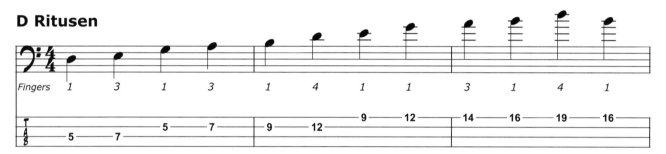

E Ritusen

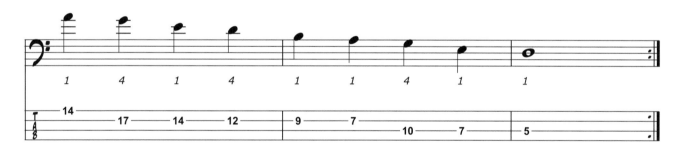

The Ritusen scale
4-string positions

F Ritusen

G Ritusen

A Ritusen

B Ritusen

C Ritusen

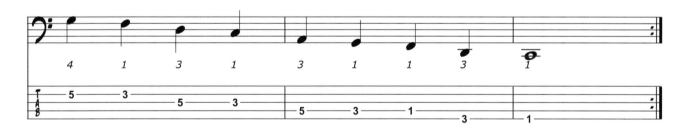

D Ritusen

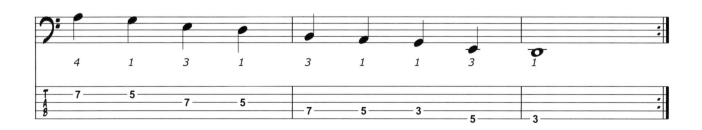

THE Egyptian scale

Construction

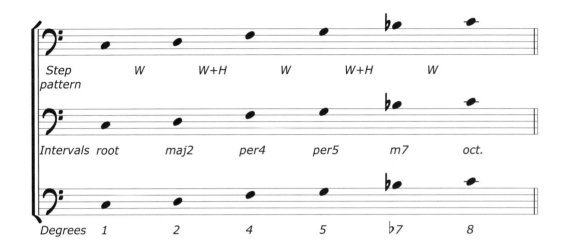

Step pattern		W	W+H	W	W+H	W	

Intervals	root	maj2	per4	per5	m7	oct.

Degrees	1	2	4	5	b7	8

Chords

(Play the scale over these chords)

CM   Csus⁴   C⁷   C⁷sus⁴   CM⁹   C¹¹   CM¹³

Related scales

(Scales with the same sound characteristics)

dorian, mixolydian, aeolian, mixolydian b6

One Octave Positions

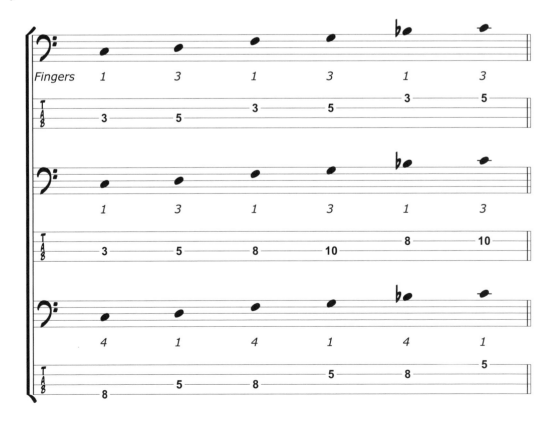

C Egyptian (Major Pentatonic - Mode 2)

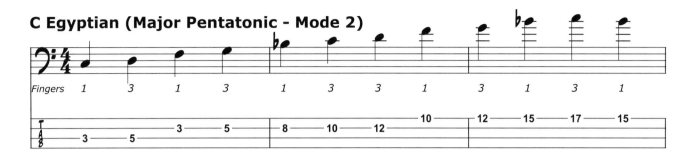

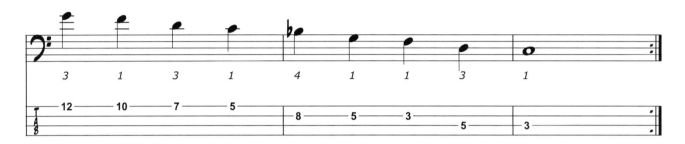

D Egyptian

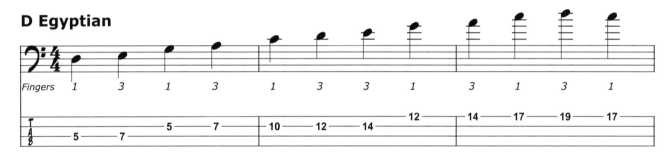

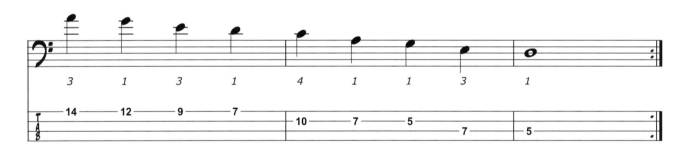

E Egyptian

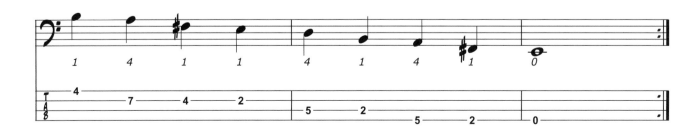

The Egyptian scale

4-string positions

B Egyptian

C Egyptian

D Egyptian

THE Iwato scale

Construction

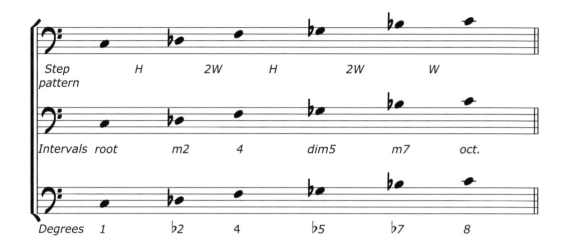

	Step pattern	H	2W	H	2W	W
Intervals	root	m2	4	dim5	m7	oct.
Degrees	1	b2	4	b5	b7	8

Chords
(Play the scale over these chords)

C°   Cm7(b5)   C7(b5)   Cm7(b5 b9)   C7(b5 b9 b13)

Related scales
(Scales with the same sound characteristics)

locrian, harmonic minor - mode 2, Spanish (eight-tone)

One Octave Positions

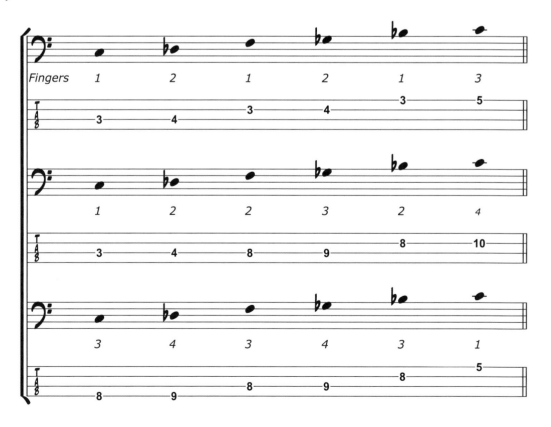

C Iwato

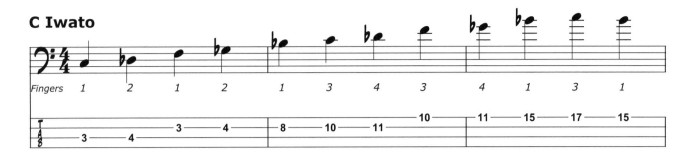

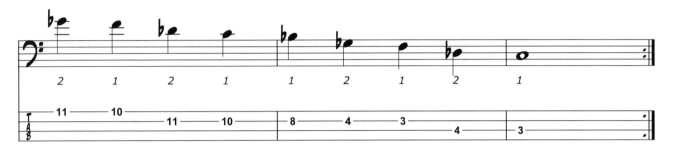

D Iwato

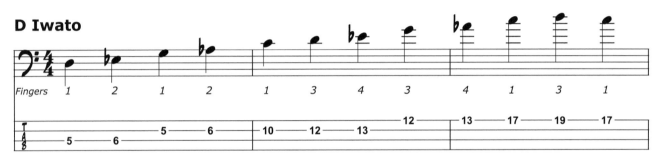

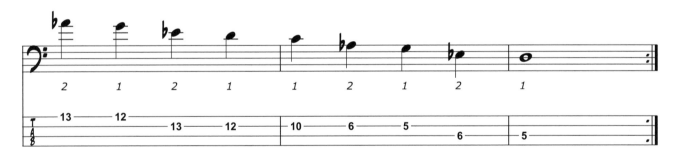

E Iwato

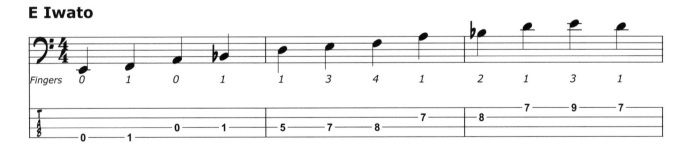

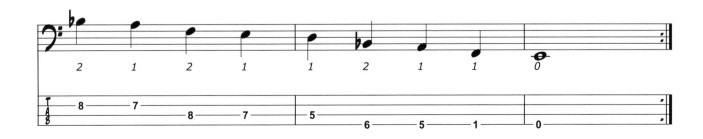

The Iwato scale
4-string positions

F Iwato

G Iwato

A Iwato

B Iwato

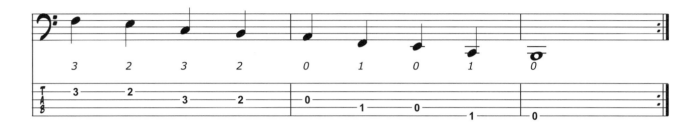

C Iwato

D Iwato

THE Japanese scale

Construction

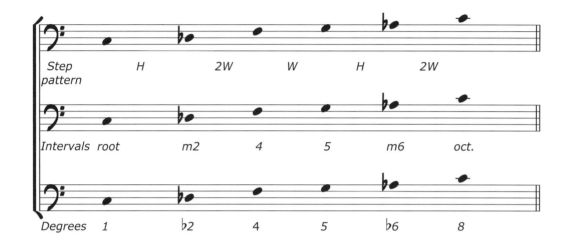

Step pattern		H	2W	W	H	2W
Intervals	root	m2	4	5	m6	oct.
Degrees	1	b2	4	5	b6	8

Chords

(Play the scale over these chords)

CM   Csus4   C7   CM7(b9)   C7(addb9 b13)

Related scales

(Scales with the same sound characteristics)

phrygian, Spanish gypsy, double harmonic, Neapolitan minor

One Octave Positions

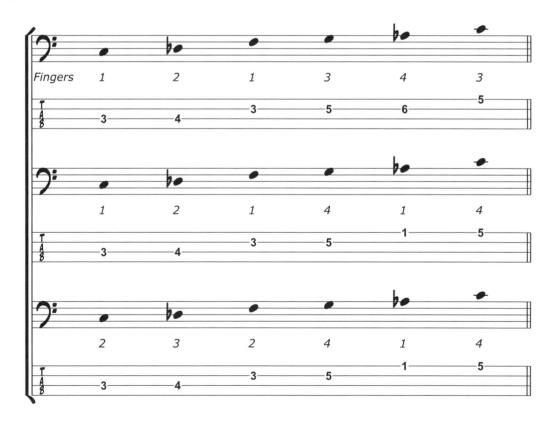

C Japanese

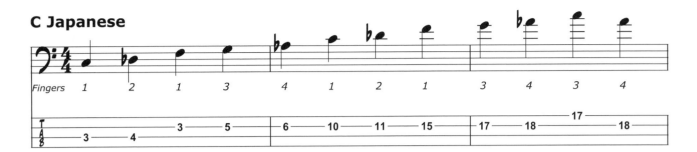

D Japanese

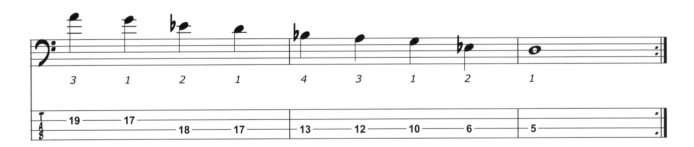

E Japanese

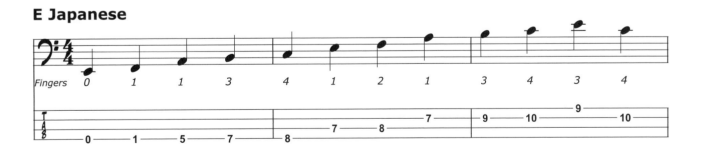

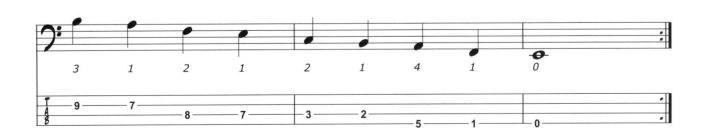

The Japanese scale
4-string positions

F Japanese

B Japanese

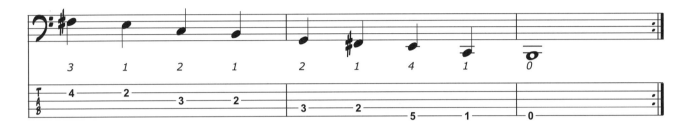

C Japanese

D Japanese

Those using
Centerstream
Books & DVDs

The Competition